ON THE EDGE

Lucasville Legends is published by Lucasville Media
an imprint of JL dub Media, Inc.
9255 Towne Centre Drive, Suite 500, San Diego, CA 92121

No part of this publication may be reproduced in whole or in part, or stored in a retrieval system, or transmitted in any form or by any means, electronic, mechanical, photocopying, recording, or otherwise, without written permission of the publisher.

For information regarding permission, write to
JL dub Media, Inc.
9255 Towne Centre Drive, Suite 500, San Diego, CA 92121
www.Lucasville.com

Lucasville is a registered trademark of JL dub Media, Inc.

Printed in the United States of America

Editorial Credits
Sal Fish, CEO/President SCORE International
Sarah M. Crookston, Reading Specialist

Photo Credits
Alexander, John. 28a
Castaneda, Luis. 29a
D&D Photography. 20b
Daily, Patrick. 24ab,27d,30c,31b,32-33
DiGiovanni, Joey. 18-19
DoubledownPhotos.com. 5,22,23abc
Dutto, Nicola. 28c
Groak, Bill. 6-7
Google Earth. 12,13
KC HiLiTES. Front cover, 2-3
Knakal, Vincent (Mad Media). 15,25ab
Lord, Andrew. 17, Back cover
MyBajaPhoto.com. 21b,29b
Pierall, Trey. 14a,16ab,25a,30a
Pritchard, Robb. 26bd,27c,30b
Rinard, Robb. 20a,21a
Tally, Scott. 10-11,26a,31a
TheGentlemanDriver.com. 28b
Trackside Photo. 8-9
Waldron, Collin. 26c
Yokohama Tire Corp. 24c,27ab,28d,30

JL dub MEDIA

Copyright © 2011 by JL dub Media, Inc.
All rights reserved.

Publisher's Cataloging-in-Publication data
Wilson, Janet L.
    Heidi's off-road truck / Janet Wilson.
    p. cm.
    ISBN 978-0-9834110-1-7
    Series : Lucasville Legends.
1. All terrain vehicle racing --Mexico --Baja California (Peninsula) --Fiction. 2. Pick-up trucks --Fiction. 3. Off road vehicles --Fiction. 4. Sport utility vehicles --Fiction. 5. All terrain vehicle racing --Mexico --Baja California (Peninsula) --Juvenile fiction. 6. Pick-up trucks --Juvenile fiction. 7. Off road vehicles --Juvenile fiction. 8. Sport utility vehicles --Juvenile fiction. I. Series. II. Title.
PZ7.W6843 He 2011
[Fic]   2011906721
The publisher does not endorse products whose logos may appear in images in this boo

Heidi's Off Road Truck

Lucasville Legends on the Edge

Janet Wilson

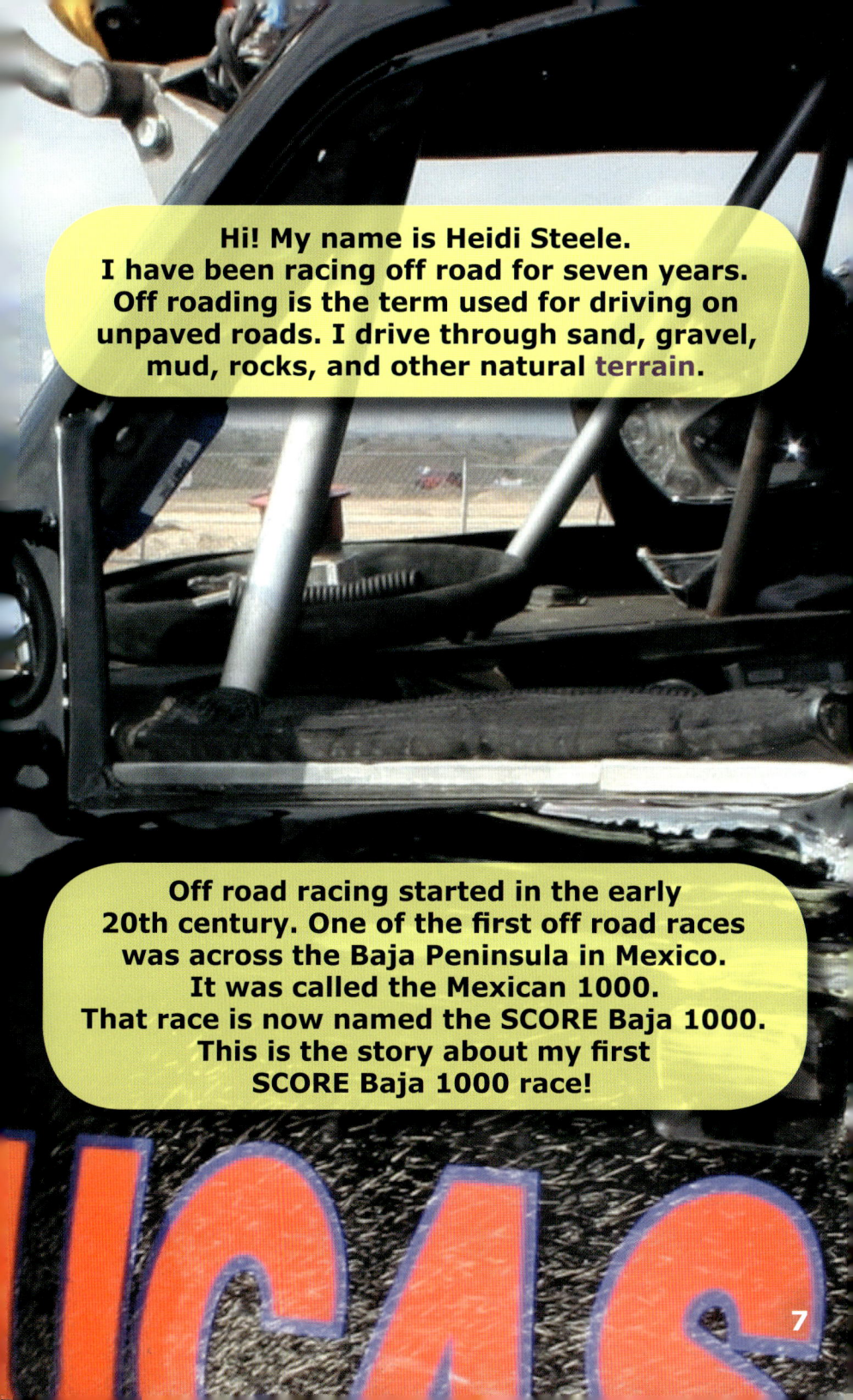

Hi! My name is Heidi Steele. I have been racing off road for seven years. Off roading is the term used for driving on unpaved roads. I drive through sand, gravel, mud, rocks, and other natural terrain.

Off road racing started in the early 20th century. One of the first off road races was across the Baja Peninsula in Mexico. It was called the Mexican 1000. That race is now named the SCORE Baja 1000. This is the story about my first SCORE Baja 1000 race!

Off Road

Body
Class 6 trucks must have a production looking body

Windows
glass removed and a safety net is installed

Spare Tires

This is my Ford Ranger Class 6 truck. Class 6 is the Production Unlimited category. "Production" means the truck's body looks like a normal truck. Something that makes my truck "unlimited" is the custom suspension.

Truck

Roll Bars
protects the driver during a crash

Grill and Headlights
standard openings must be retained

Suspension
raised for extra ground clearance

The cockpit of my truck does not look like a production truck. The side windows are replaced with nets and the steering wheel can be removed.

The navigators, Pancho and Richie use the GPS unit. During the race, they will talk to our support crews using the two-way radio.

The seat belts are 5-point harnesses. Roll bars have been added to the structure. This extra safety equipment will help to protect us in case of a crash.

Loop Race
The race starts and finishes in Ensenada, Baja California.

The SCORE Baja 1000 takes place in November on Mexico's Baja California **Peninsula**. The course changes every year. Some years the race course is huge loop. Other years, the course is a point-to-point race. A point-to-point race is also known as a "**Peninsula** Run".

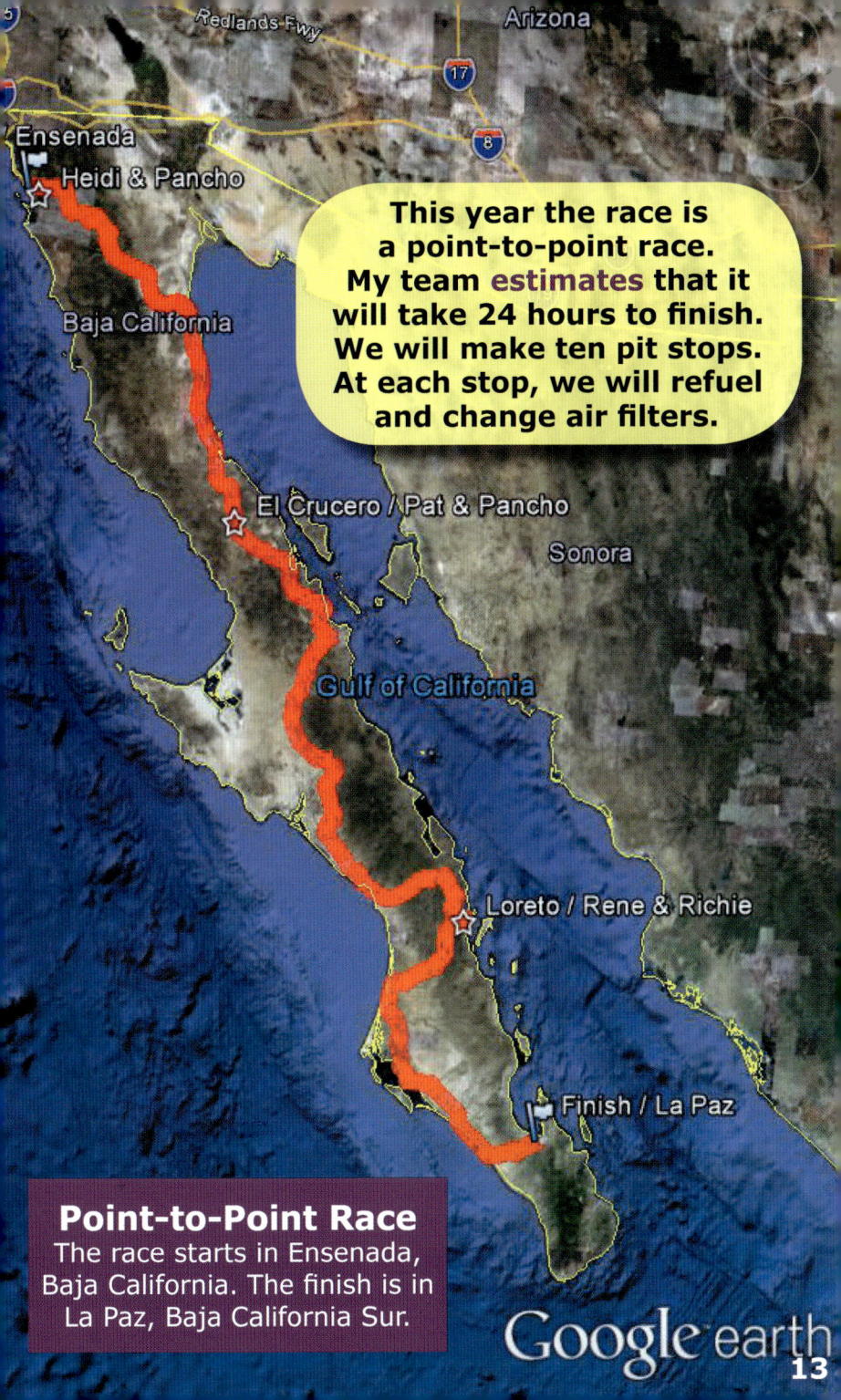

This year the race is a point-to-point race. My team **estimates** that it will take 24 hours to finish. We will make ten pit stops. At each stop, we will refuel and change air filters.

Point-to-Point Race
The race starts in Ensenada, Baja California. The finish is in La Paz, Baja California Sur.

Everyone asks, "Are you ready?" I reply "Yes! I'm always ready to throw some dirt!"

All of the vehicles must be inspected. This inspection occurs the day before the race. The teams form a line down the street. This line is called Contingency Row.

Contingency Row

Contingency Row is busy. Thousands of fans come to view the trucks and visit with the drivers. Everyone wishes us good luck.

Race Day

This is the big day! One last interview and then it is time to get ready. My heart is pounding.

I use duct tape to secure the radio into my ears. An added benefit is that the tape helps keep the dust out of my ears!

Racing in the desert for 24 hours is tiring. My team has three drivers and two navigators. Pat and I will drive the first two shifts with Pancho navigating. Rene will drive to the finish with Richie navigating. Pat and I will meet the team at the finish line in La Paz.

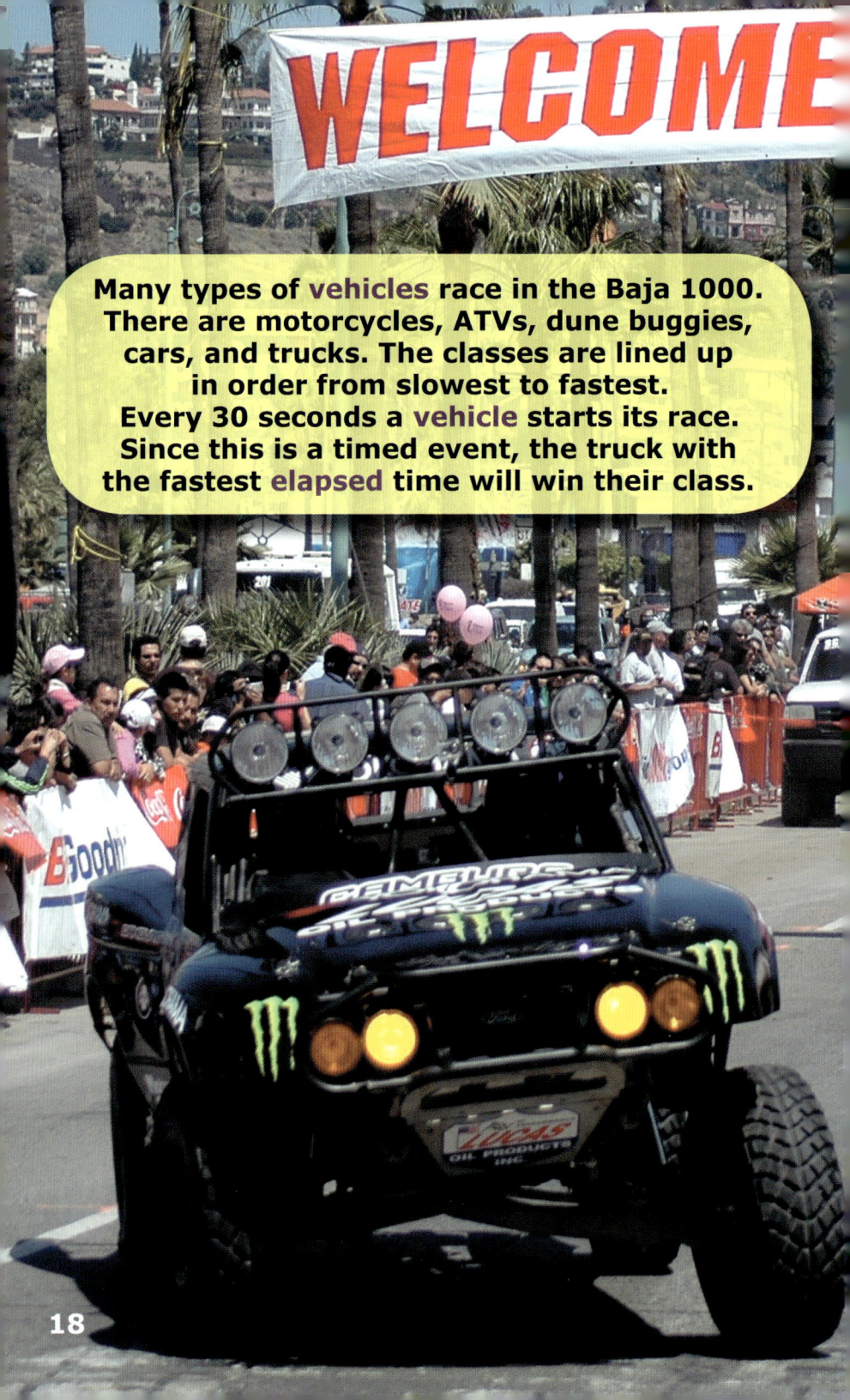

Many types of vehicles race in the Baja 1000. There are motorcycles, ATVs, dune buggies, cars, and trucks. The classes are lined up in order from slowest to fastest. Every 30 seconds a vehicle starts its race. Since this is a timed event, the truck with the fastest elapsed time will win their class.

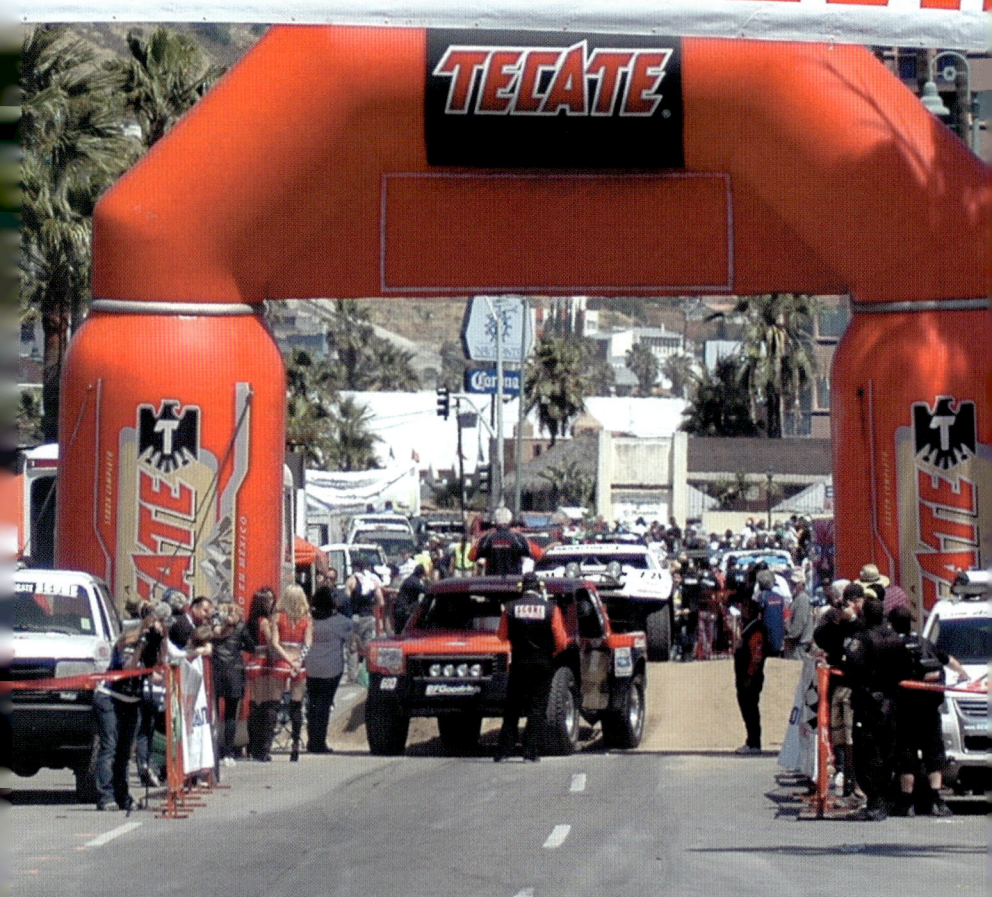

The crowd is yelling and cheering.
Finally, it is our turn. Here we go!
Pancho is navigating and talking to the crew.
We are 30 seconds behind the truck in front.

Wow! Hundreds of **spectators** are here to watch the start. Look at all the dust!

I have caught up to the truck in front of me. I will try to pass at the next wide corner.

Whoa! Watch out!

Racing in the desert is dusty . . . and full of surprises!

21

We have been racing for five hours.
I try to steer around the bigger rocks and holes.
By watching the dust clouds, we can tell that
we are gaining on the truck in front of us.

23

At each stop, my crew fills up the 45-gallon tank. The air filter is always changed because it is so dusty. The suspension is checked too.

Is everything OK?

Good! Let's go!

The truck is running great.

Racing in the desert is challenging. I listen carefully to Pancho's directions and focus on driving as fast as I can. I must stay alert because I never know what will be around the next hill.

Holy cow!

Hitting that cow would have created a huge mess!

Desert racing *is* full of surprises.

We are gaining on the truck in front of us.

What a long day. The next pit stop is El Crucero where Pat will take over driving.

Many spectators are watching this pit stop.

The crew has done a great job.

Pat honks the horn as he and Pancho race off into the night!

27

The sunrise is beautiful. The good news is that we have made it through the night without any mechanical failures.

The next pit stop is in Loreto. The crew is waiting with fuel, tires, and cold water.

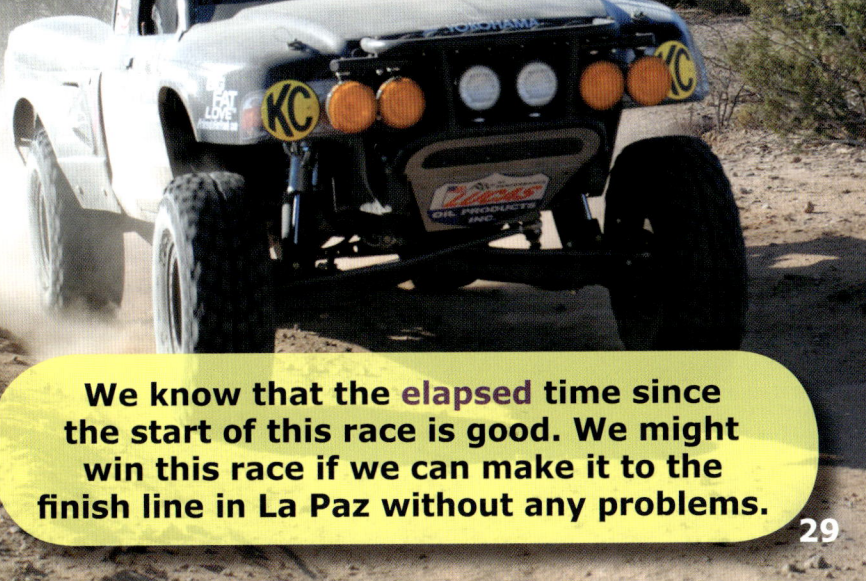

The crew fills the tank and checks the tires. Rene and Richie climb into the truck. They are heading for the finish line. Go Rene! Go Richie!

We know that the **elapsed** time since the start of this race is good. We might win this race if we can make it to the finish line in La Paz without any problems.

WOW! We won!

Everyone is so happy.

This team is so crazy that we all kiss the truck!

The race announcer interviews me.
What a wild day and night this has been.

Richie, Rene, Heidi, Patrick, and Pancho
(navigator, driver, driver, driver, and navigator)

LUCASVILLE Legends ON THE EDGE

Vocabulary

announcer [*uh*-**NOUN**-ser] - a person who reads the news on radio or television

benefit [**BEN**-*uh*-fit] - something that is good

elapse [ih-**LAPS**] - the passage of a period of time

estimate [**ES**-t*uh*-meyt] - to form an approximate judgment or opinion

inspection [in-**SPEK**-sh*uh*'n] - the official act of viewing, especially carefully or critically

mechanical [muh-**KAN**-i-k*uh*'l] - being a machine; concerned with machines

navigator [**NAV**-i-gey-ter] - a person who is skilled at reading maps and following directions

peninsula [p*uh*-**NIN**-s*uh*-l*uh*] - a strip of land projecting into a sea or lake from the mainland

spectator [**SPEK**-tey-ter] - a person who looks on or watches; onlooker; observer

suspension [suh-**SPEN**-sh*uh*'n] - a system of springs and shock absorbers that support the body of a wheeled vehicle

terrain [tuh-**REYN**] - land, especially with reference to its natural features

vehicle [**VEE**-i-k*uh*'l] - a conveyance moving on wheels in which people or objects are transported